The Essential CLASSICAL GUITAR Collection

Arranged by Alexander Glüklikh
("Für Elise" and "Canon in D" arranged by Simon Salz)

Editor: Aaron Stang
Design: Lisa Greene Mane
Artwork Reproduced on Cover: "Girl Playing Guitar" by Auguste Renoir

WARNER BROS. PUBLICATIONS - THE GLOBAL LEADER IN PRINT
USA: 15800 NW 48th Avenue, Miami, FL 33014

WARNER/CHAPPELL MUSIC

CANADA: 85 SCARSDALE ROAD, SUITE 101
DON MILLS, ONTARIO, M3B 2R2
SCANDINAVIA: P.O. BOX 533, VENDEVAGEN 85 B
S-182 15, DANDERYD, SWEDEN
AUSTRALIA: P.O. BOX 353
3 TALAVERA ROAD, NORTH RYDE N.S.W. 2113

NUOVA CARISCH

ITALY: VIA CAMPANIA, 12
20098 S. GIULIANO MILANESE (MI)
ZONA INDUSTRIALE SESTO ULTERIANO
SPAIN: MAGALLANES, 25
28015 MADRID
FRANCE: 25 RUE DE HAUTEVILLE, 75010 PARIS

INTERNATIONAL MUSIC PUBLICATIONS LIMITED

ENGLAND: SOUTHEND ROAD,
WOODFORD GREEN, ESSEX IG8 8HN
GERMANY: MARSTALLSTR. 8, D-80539 MUNCHEN
DENMARK: DANMUSIK, VOGNMAGERGADE 7
DK 1120 KOBENHAVNK

CONTENTS

COMPOSER INDEX

4

AIR

Music by
JEAN-BAPTISTE LULLY
Arranged by
ALEXANDER GLÜKLIKH

Allegro Moderato (♩ = 80)

Air - 2 - 1

ANDANTE

Music by
CHRISTOPH WILLIBALD GLÜCK
Arranged by **ALEXANDER GLÜKLIKH**

Andante - 2 - 1

Andante - 2 - 2

ARABESQUE

CLAUDE DEBUSSY
Arranged by
ALEXANDER GLÜKLIKH

Arabesque - 2 - 1

AVE MARIA

FRANZ SCHUBERT
Arranged by
ALEXANDER GLÜKLIKH

Ave Maria - 2 - 1

Ave Maria - 2 - 2

AVE MARIA

By BACH/GOUNOD
Arranged by
ALEXANDER GLÜKLIKH

Andante con moto ♩ = 76

Ave Maria - 2 - 1

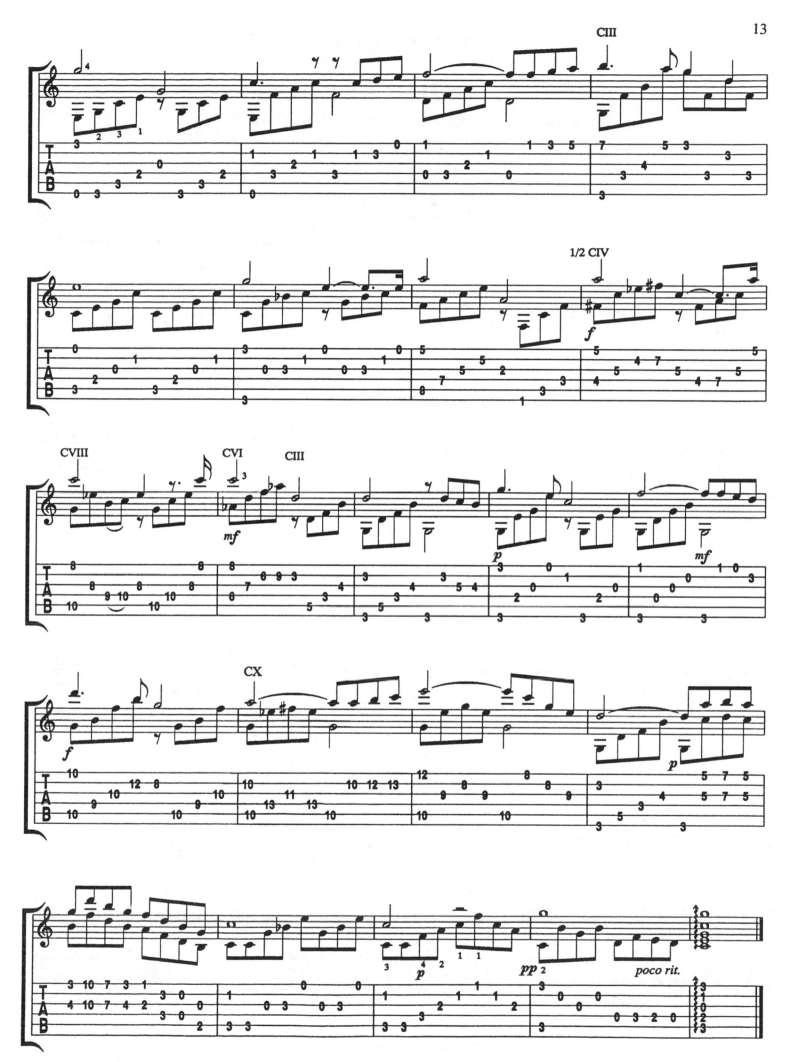

BOURRÉE
From the First Lute Suite in E Minor (BMV996)

J.S. BACH
Arranged by MIKE BRIGGS

*Not on original score - may have been implied in this period. Please use your discretion.

Bourrée –2 –1

Bourrée –2 –2

AMADIS DE GRECE

Music by
ANDRE DESTOUCHES
Arranged by
ALEXANDER GLÜKLIKH

CANON IN D
"Pachelbel's Canon"

by JOHANN PACHELBEL
Arranged by SIMON SALZ

*Chord pattern repeats every four bars.

Canon in D - 3 - 1

CLAIR DE LUNE

CLAUDE DEBUSSY
Arranged by
ALEXANDER GLÜKLIKH

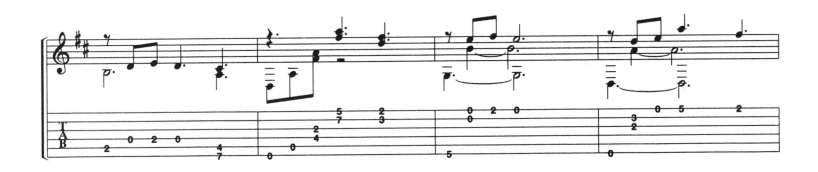

Clair de Lune - 3 - 1

Clair de Lune - 3 - 2

22

CZARDAS

V. MONTI
Arranged by
ALEXANDER GLÜKLIKH

Czardas - 3 - 1

Czardas - 3 - 2

Czardas - 3 - 3

DARK EYES
(Variations on a Theme)

RUSSIAN FOLK SONG
Arranged by
ALEXANDER GLÜKLIKH

Dark Eyes – 4 – 1

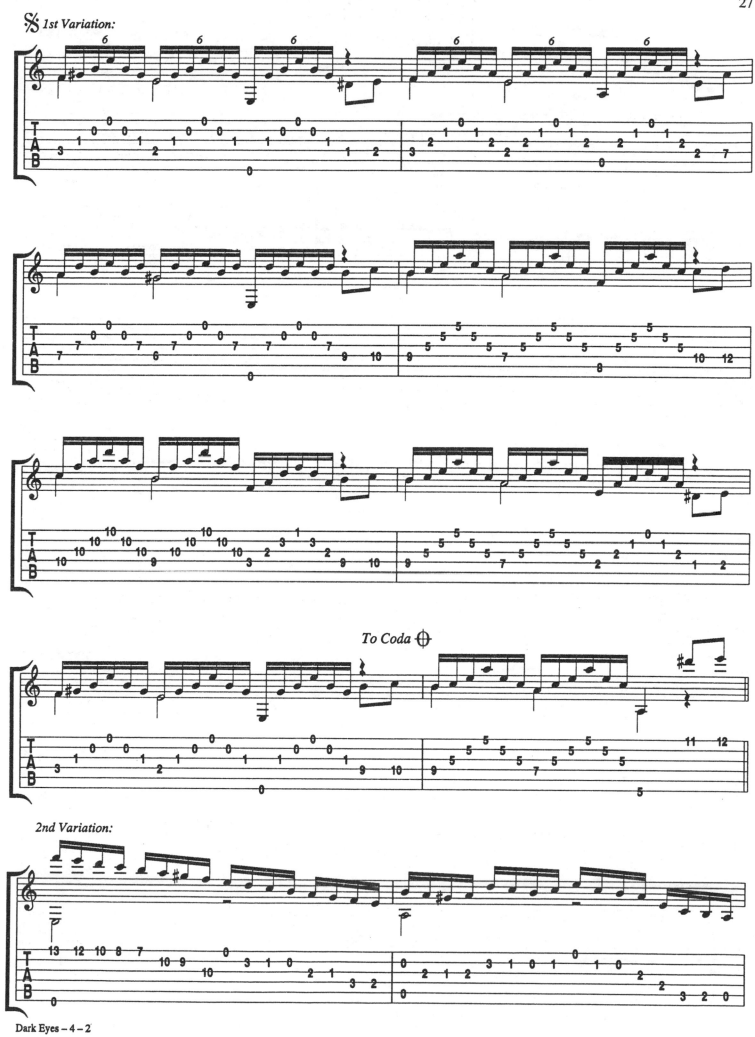

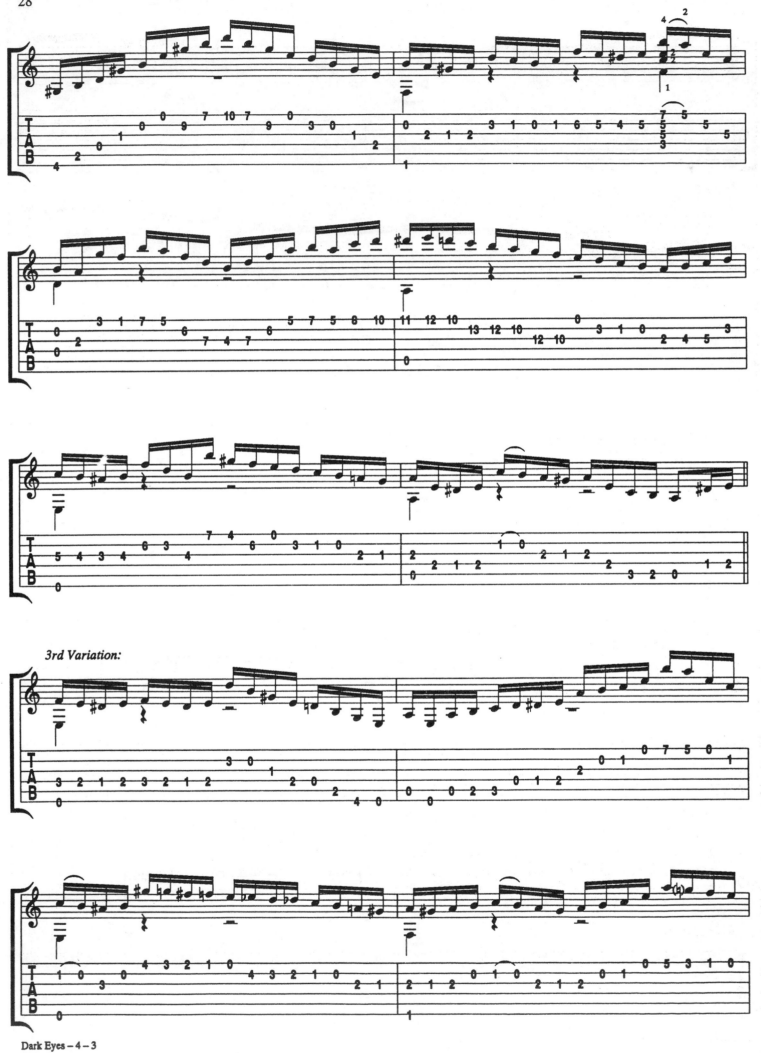

3rd Variation:

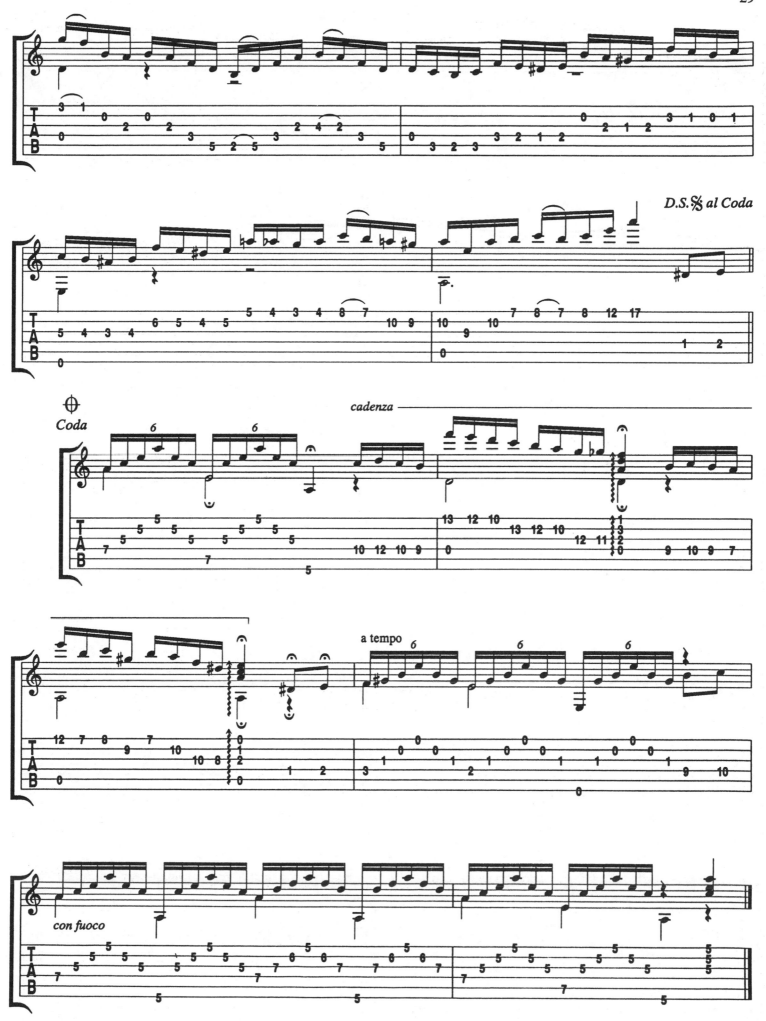

Dark Eyes – 4 – 4

DOUBLE

J.S. BACH
Arranged by
ALEXANDER GLÜKLIKH

Double - 2 - 1

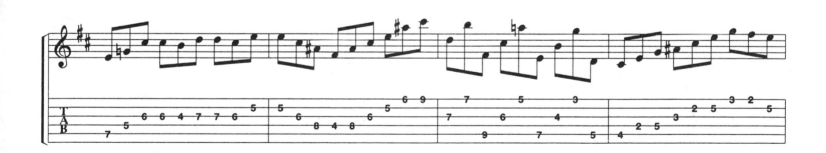

Double - 2 - 2

ENTR'ACTE

Music by
FRANZ SCHUBERT
Arranged by
ALEXANDER GLÜKLIKH

CHOPIN ETUDE

FREDERIC CHOPIN
Arranged by
ALEXANDER GLÜKLIKH

Etude - 3 - 1

Etude - 3 - 2

FANTASIE IMPROMPTU

FREDERIC CHOPIN
Arranged by
ALEXANDER GLÜKLIKH

Fantasie Impromptu - 2 - 1

VII

Fantasie Impromptu -2 - 2

FLIGHT OF THE BUMBLE BEE

NIKOLAI RIMSKY-KORSAKOV
Arranged by
ALEXANDER GLÜKLIKH

⑥=D

Presto ♩ = 150

Flight of the Bumble Bee - 4 - 1

Flight of the Bumble Bee -4 - 2

Flight of the Bumble Bee - 4 - 4

FADED PAGE

Music by
NICOLAI MIASKOVSKY
Arranged by
ALEXANDER GLÜKLIKH

THE FOUR SEASONS

(A Suite of Themes)
Theme from "SUMMER" Op. 8, No. 2
Movt. 1

ANTONIO VIVALDI
Arranged by
ALEXANDER GLÜKLIKH

The Four Seasons – 7 – 1

Theme from "SPRING" Op. 8, No. 1
Movt. 1

ANTONIO VIVALDI
Arranged by
ALEXANDER GLÜKLIKH

Theme from "AUTUMN" Op. 8, No. 3
Movt. 1

ANTONIO VIVALDI
Arranged by
ALEXANDER GLÜKLIKH

Allegro (♩ = 100 - 104)

The Four Seasons - 7 - 5

Theme from "WINTER" Op. 8, No. 4
Movt. 2

ANTONIO VIVALDI
Arranged by
ALEXANDER GLÜKLIKH

The Four Seasons – 7 – 7

FÜR ELISE

LUDWIG VAN BEETHOVEN
Arranged by SIMON SALZ

Für Elise – 5 – 2

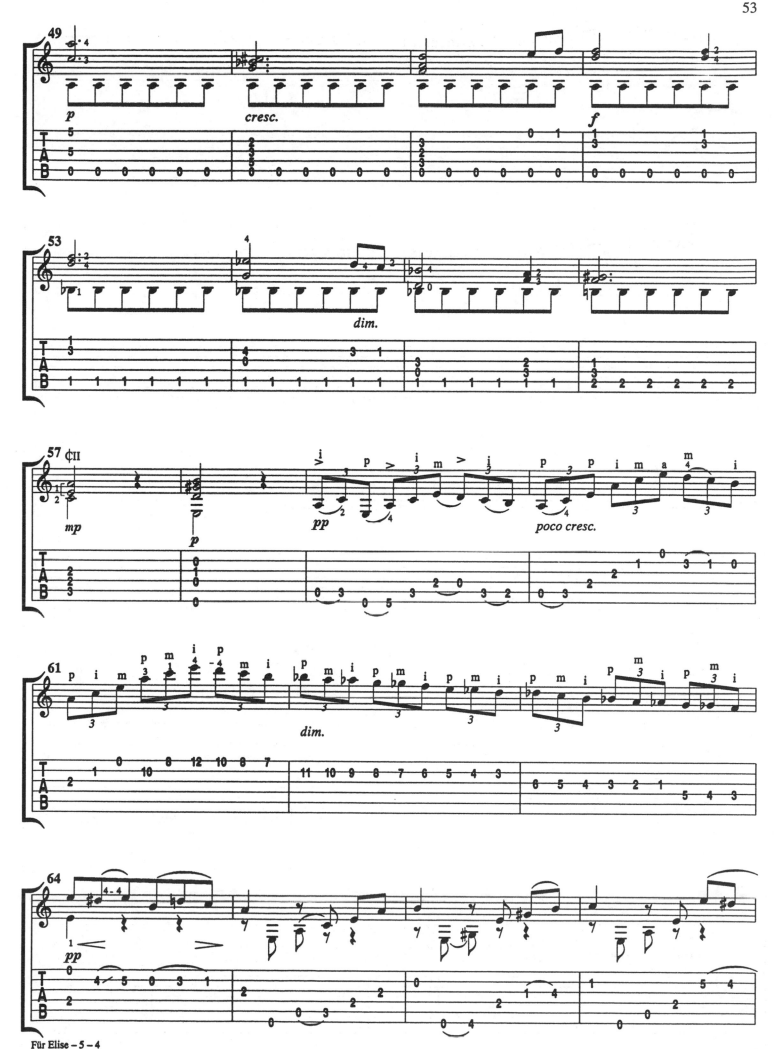

MOONLIGHT SONATA

LUDWIG VAN BEETHOVEN
Arranged by
ALEXANDER GLÜKLIKH

Adagio sostenuto ♩ = 53

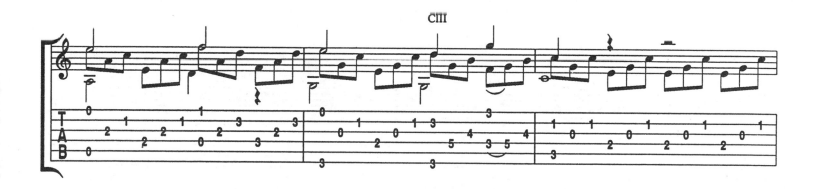

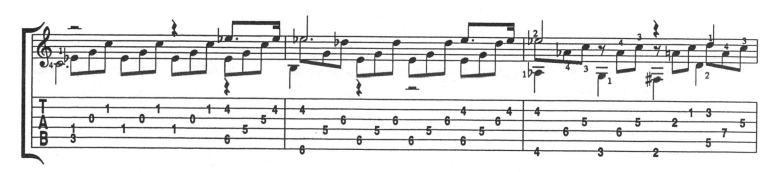

Moonlight Sonata – 5 – 1

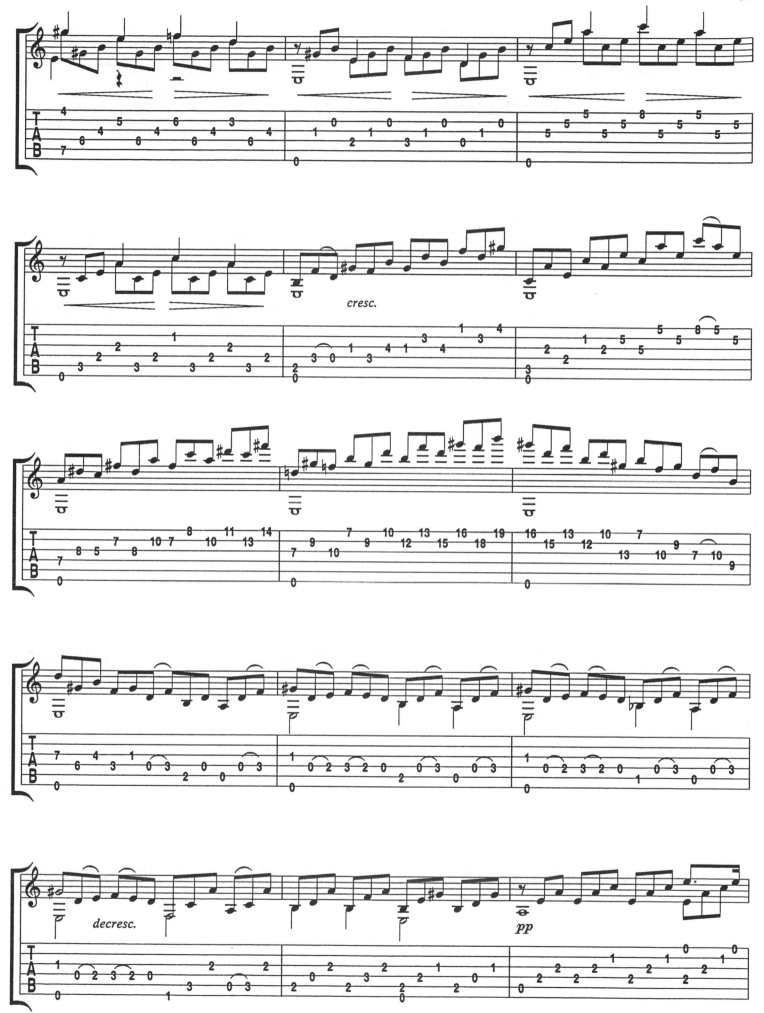

Moonlight Sonata – 5 – 3

58

Moonlight Sonata – 5 – 5

GREENSLEEVES

ANONYMOUS
(16th Century)
Arranged by ALEXANDER GLÜKLIKH

Gently flowing ♩ = 120

Greensleeves – 2 – 1

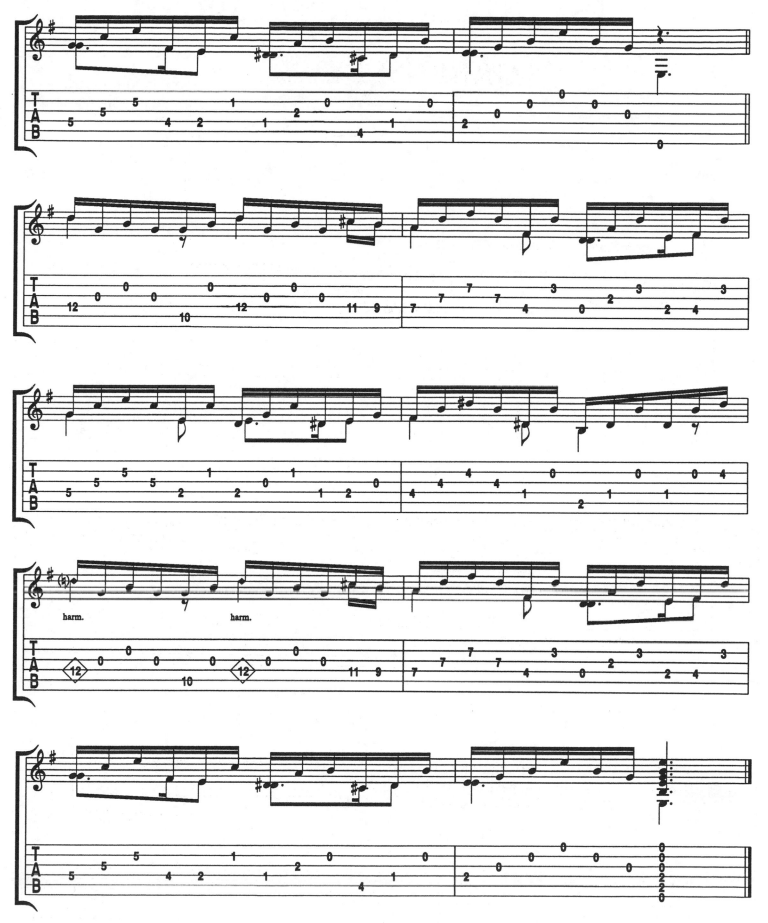

Greensleeves – 2 – 2

JESU, JOY OF MAN'S DESIRING

By JOHANN SEBASTIAN BACH
Arranged by SIMON SALZ

Jesu, Joy of Man's Desiring - 4 - 1

Jesu, Joy of Man's Desiring - 4 - 2

*use knuckle

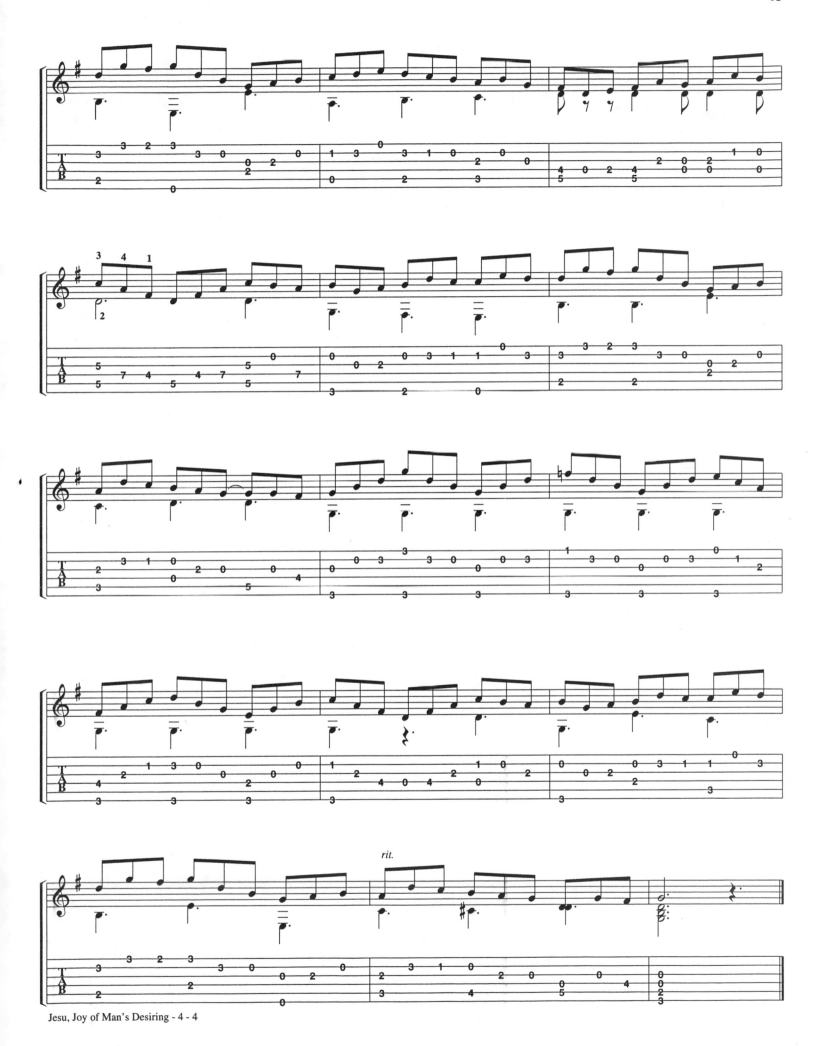

Jesu, Joy of Man's Desiring - 4 - 4

JUNE
(Barcarolle)

Music by
PETER ILYICH TCHAIKOVSKY
Arranged by
ALEXANDER GLÜKLIKH

Andante cantabile (♩ = 92 - 96)

June - 4 - 1

MY HEART AT THY SWEET VOICE

Music by
CAMILLE SAINT-SAENS
Arranged by
ALEXANDER GLÜKLIKH

My Heart At Thy Sweet Voice - 2 - 1

My Heart At Thy Sweet Voice - 2 - 2

PAVANE

Music by
GABRIEL FAURE
Arranged by
ALEXANDER GLÜKLIKH

Pavane - 2 - 1

Pavane - 2 - 2

PAVANE
(Pour Une Infante Défunte)

MAURICE RAVEL
Arranged by
ALEXANDER GLÜKLIKH

Pavane (Pour Une Infante Défunte) - 2 - 1

Pavane (Pour Une Infante Défunte) - 2 - 2

PRELUDE No. 1

J.S. BACH
Arranged by
ALEXANDER GLÜKLIKH

CII

Prelude No. 1 - 3 - 3

REVERIE

Music by
PETER ILYICH TCHAIKOVSKY
Arranged by
ALEXANDER GLÜKLIKH

Reverie - 3 - 1

81

Reverie - 3 - 3

ROMANCE

Music by
ANTON RUBINSTEIN
Arranged by
ALEXANDER GLÜKLIKH

Andante con moto (♩ = 80)

Romance - 3 - 1

83

Romance - 3 - 2

ROMANCE

Music by
ROBERT SCHUMANN
Arranged by
ALEXANDER GLÜKLIKH

ROMANZA

ANONYMOUS
(19th Century)
Arranged by ALEXANDER GLÜKLIKH

Moderato ♩ = 88

Romanza – 5 – 1

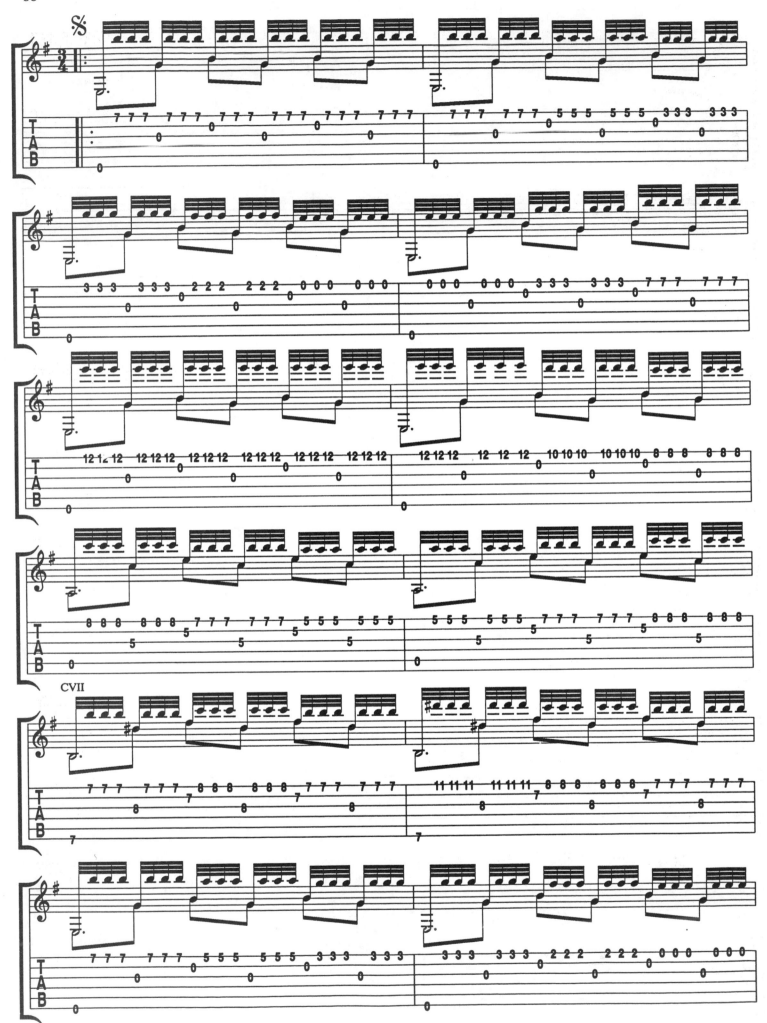

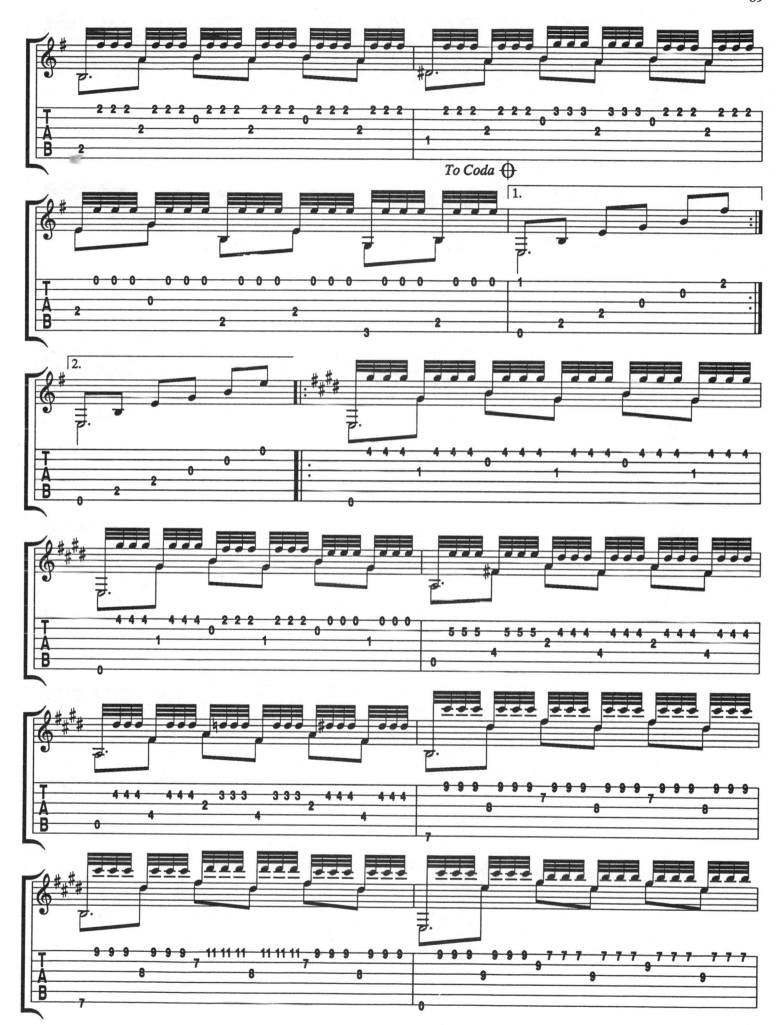

To Coda ⊕

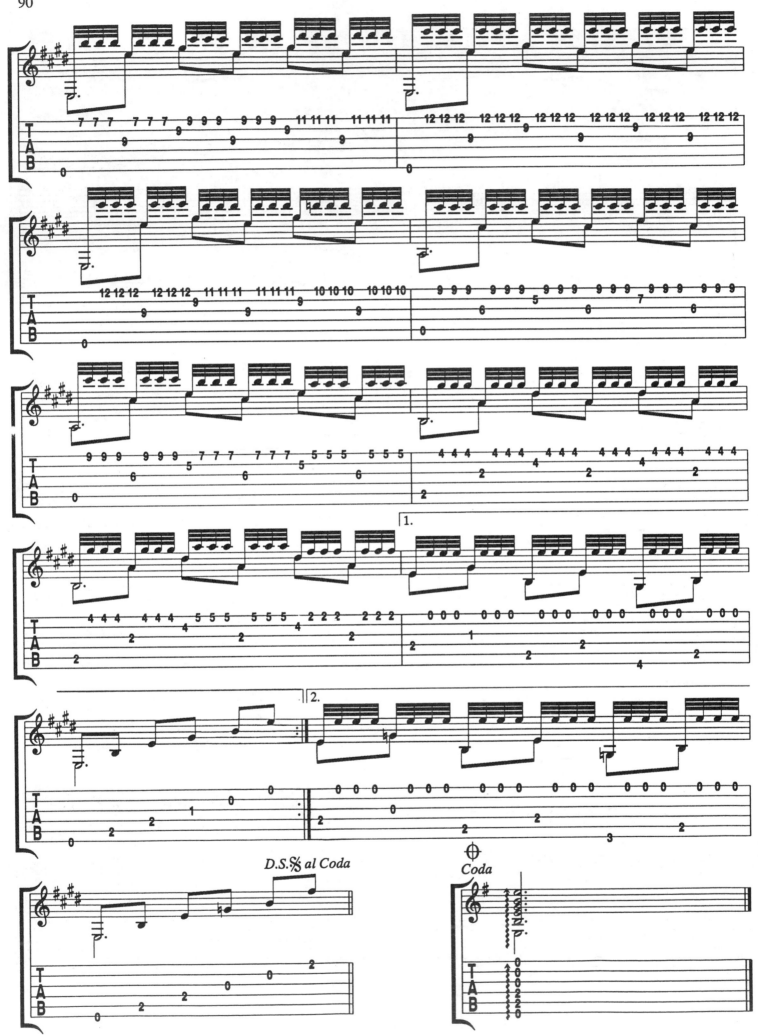

THE SWAN

CAMILLE SAINT-SAËNS
Arranged by ALEXANDER GLÜKLIKH

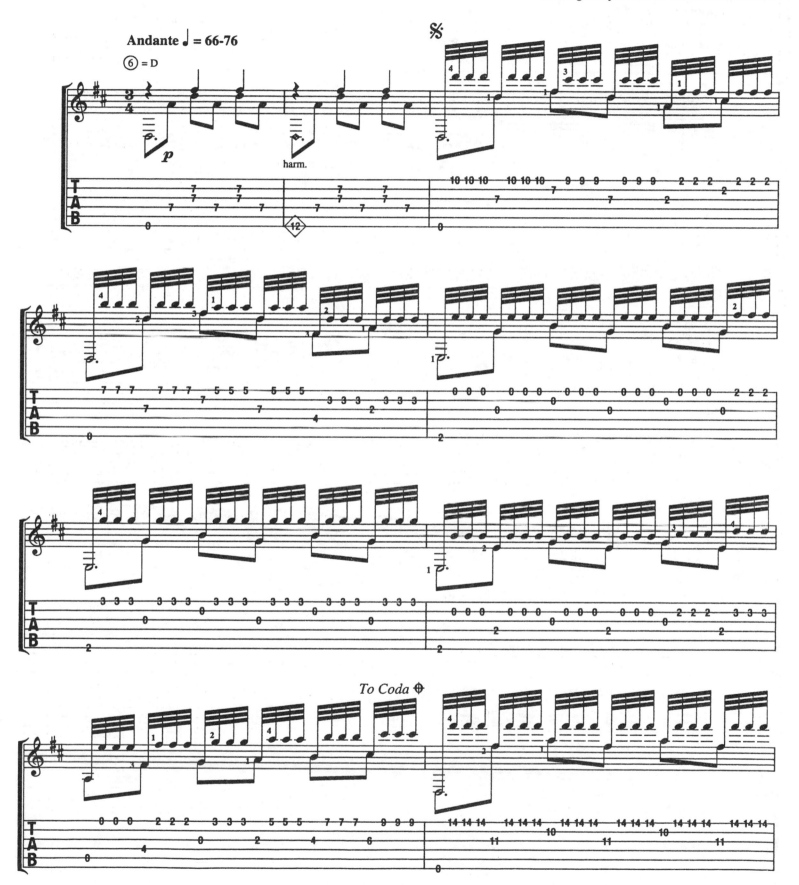

The Swan - 5 - 1

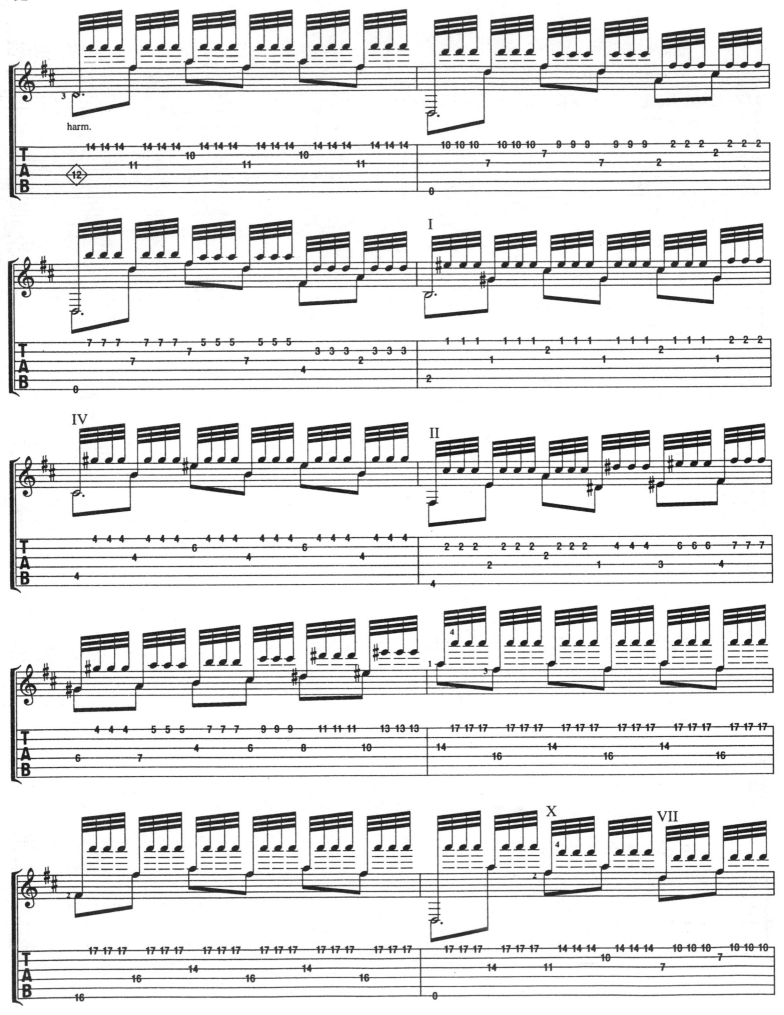

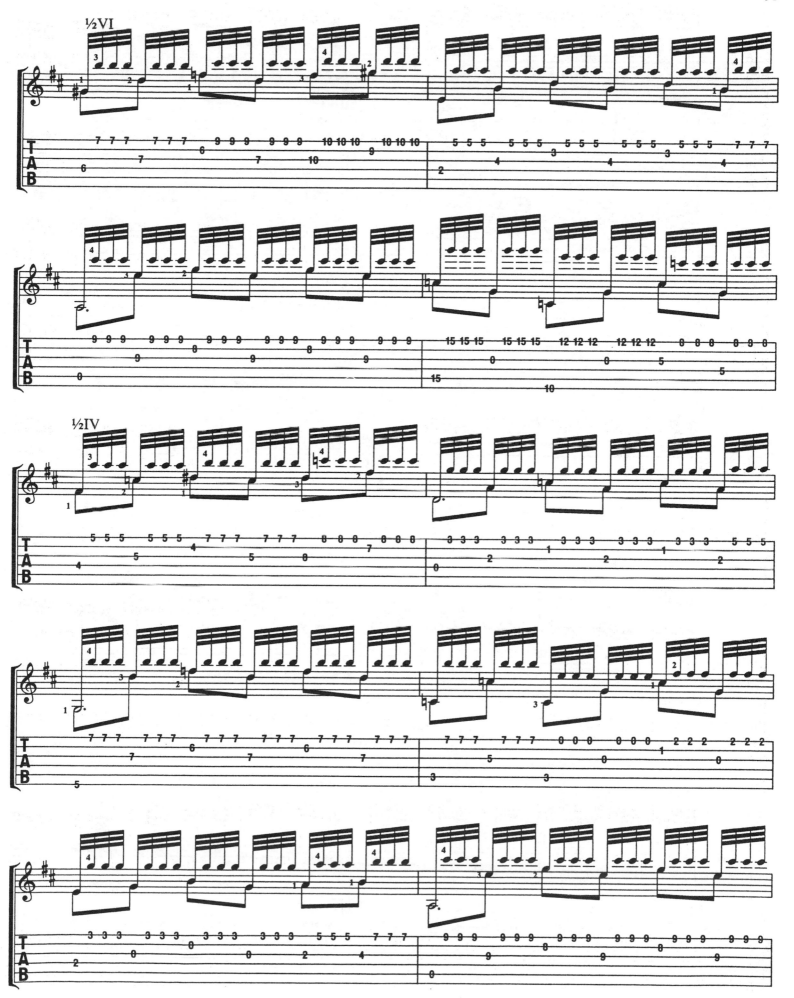

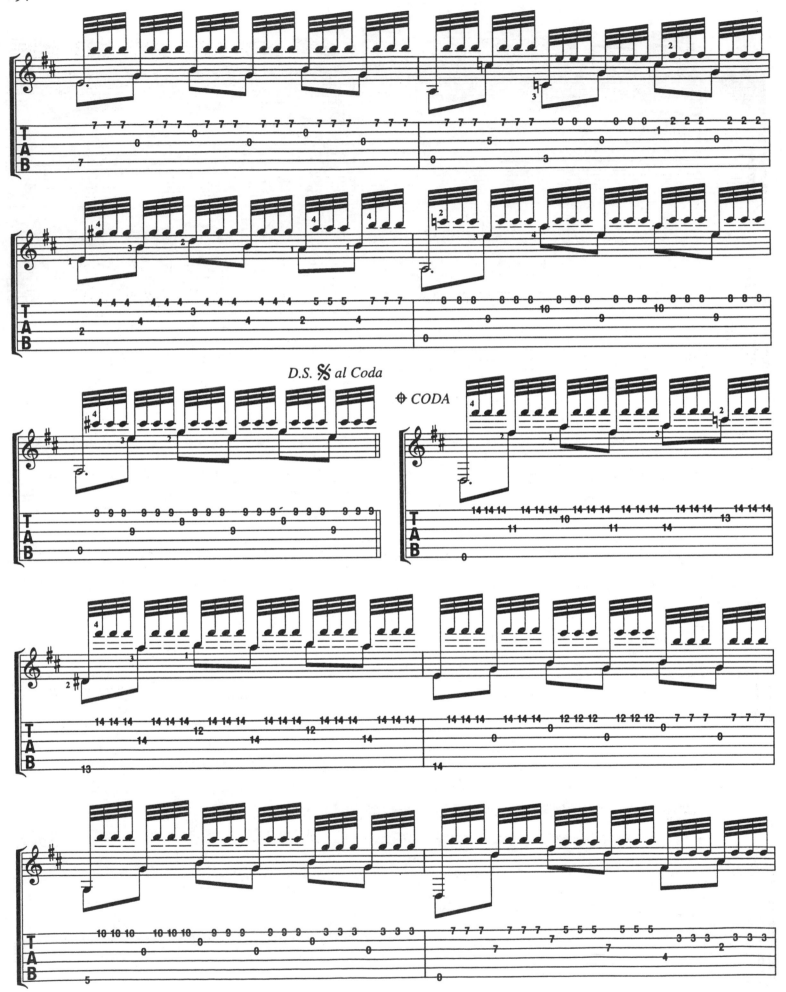

D.S. 𝄋 al Coda

⊕ CODA

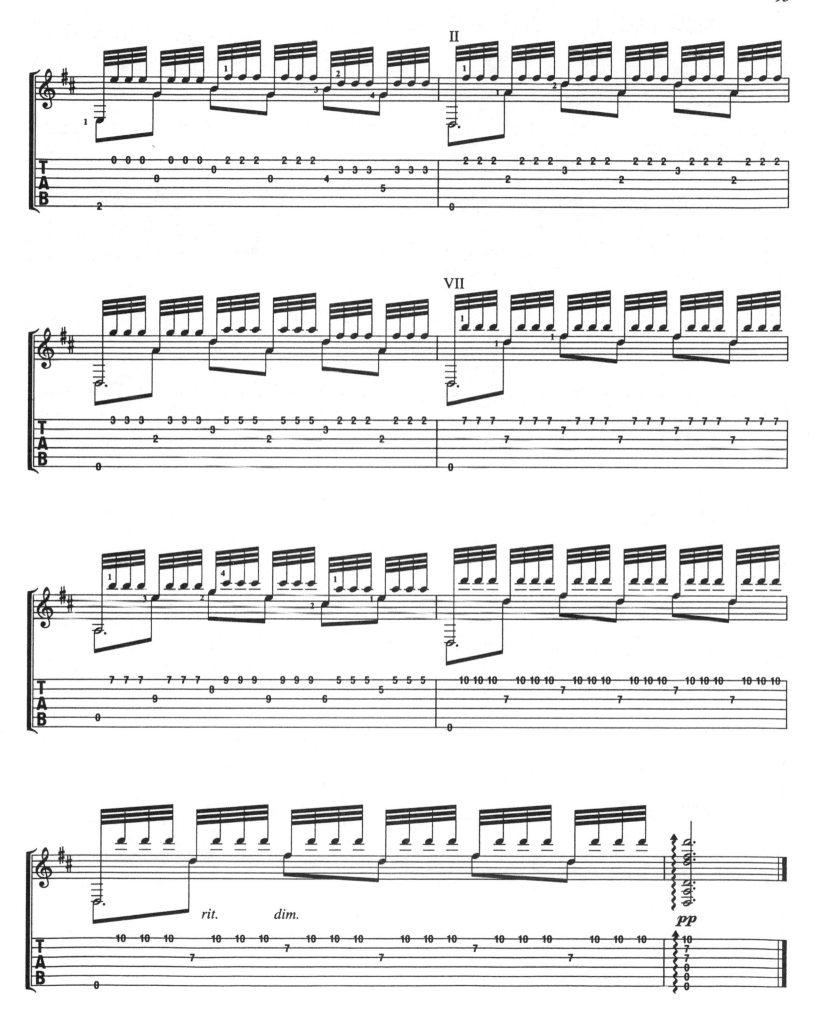

SARABANDA

J.S. BACH
Arranged by
ALEXANDER GLÜKLIKH

Sarabanda - 2 - 1

Sarabanda - 2 - 2

SICILIANO
From Sonata No. 2 for the Flute and Harpsichord

J.S. BACH
Arranged by
ALEXANDER GLÜKLIKH

Siciliano - 2 - 1

Siciliano - 2 - 2

SICILIENNE

Music by
GABRIEL FAURE
Arranged by
ALEXANDER GLÜKLIKH

Sicilienne - 2 - 1

TWO GUITARS

TRADITIONAL
Arranged by
ALEXANDER GLÜKLIKH

Two Guitars - 3 - 1